The Type

The Type

Sarah Kay

Illustrated by Sophia Janowitz

hachette
BOOKS

NEW YORK   BOSTON

Hachette Books
Hachette Book Group
1290 Avenue of the Americas
New York, NY 10104
HachetteBookGroup.com

Printed in the United States of America

Phoenix Color

First edition: February 2016
10 9 8 7 6 5 4 3 2 1

Hachette Books is a division of Hachette Book Group, Inc.
The Hachette Books name and logo are trademarks of Hachette Book Group, Inc.

The publisher is not responsible for websites (or their content) that are not owned by the publisher.

ISBN: 978-0-316-38660-9

Everyone needs a place. It shouldn't be inside of someone else.
                                                    —Richard Siken

If you grow up the type of woman men want to look at,
you can let them look at you.

Do not mistake eyes for hands.
Or windows. Or mirrors.

Let them see what a woman looks like.
They may not have ever seen one before.

If you grow up the type of woman men want to touch,

you can let them touch you.

Sometimes it is not you they are reaching for.
Sometimes it is a bottle. A door. A sandwich.

A Pulitzer. Another woman.
But their hands found you first.

Do not mistake yourself for a guardian.

Or a muse.
Or a promise.
Or a victim.
Or a snack.

You are a woman.
Skin and bones.
Veins and nerves.
Hair and sweat.

You are not made of metaphors.
Not apologies.
Not excuses.

If you grow up the type of woman men want to hold,
you can let them hold you.

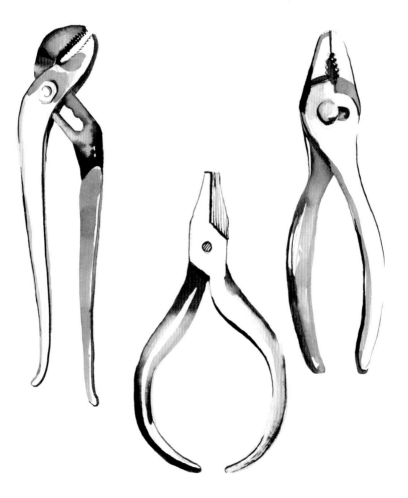

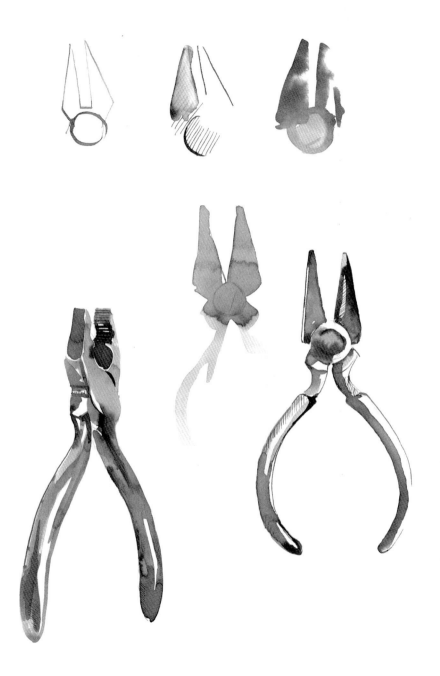

All day they practice keeping their bodies upright—
even after all this evolving, it still feels unnatural,

still pulls tight the muscles, strains the arms and spine.

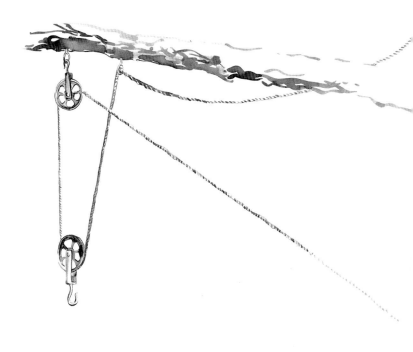

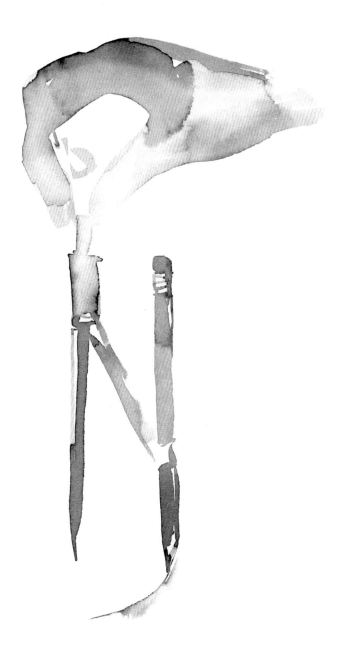

Only some men want to learn what it feels like
to wrap themselves into a question mark around you,

admit they do not have the answers
they thought they would have by now;

some men will want to hold you like The Answer.

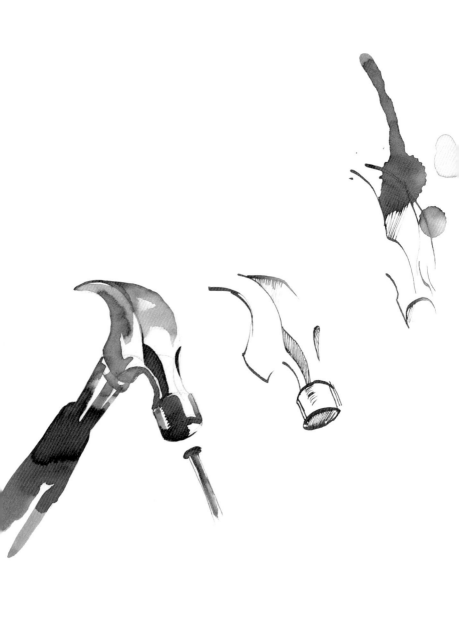

You are not The Answer.

You are not the problem.

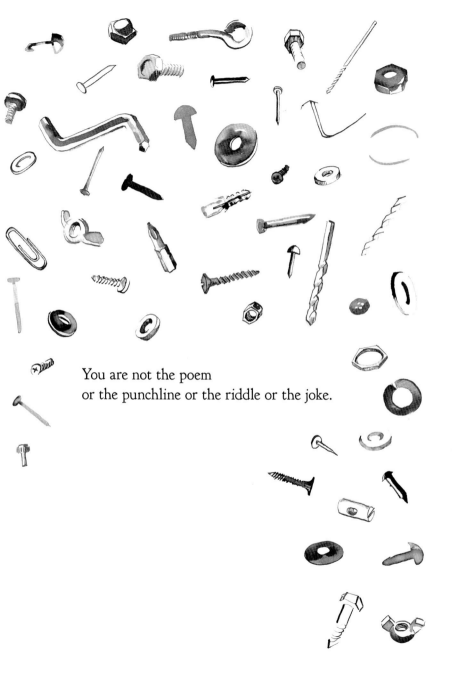

You are not the poem
or the punchline or the riddle or the joke.

Woman. If you grow up the type men want to love, you can let them love you.

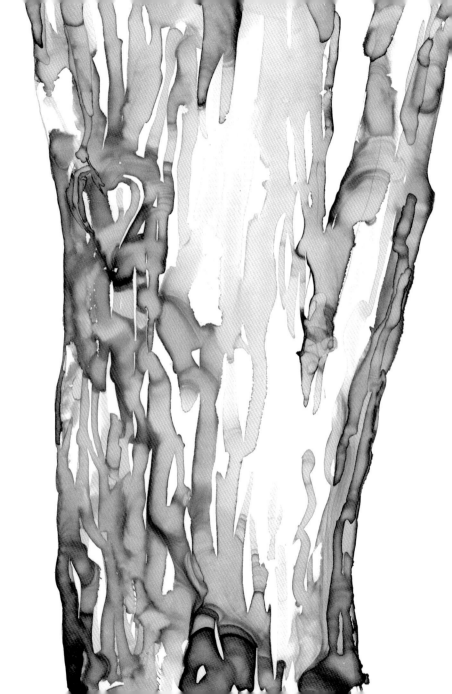

Being loved is not the same thing as loving.

When you fall in love, it is discovering the ocean after years of puddle jumping.

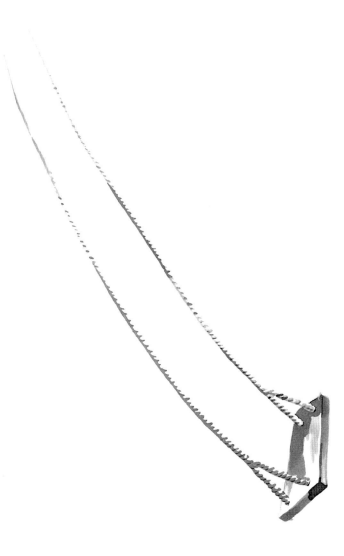

It is realizing you have hands.

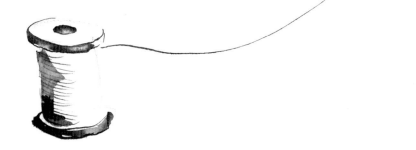

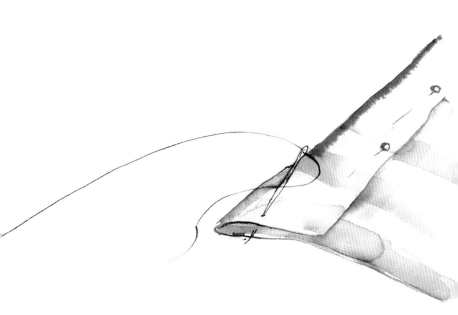

It is reaching for the tightrope
when the crowds have all gone home.

Do not spend time wondering if you are
the type of woman men will hurt.

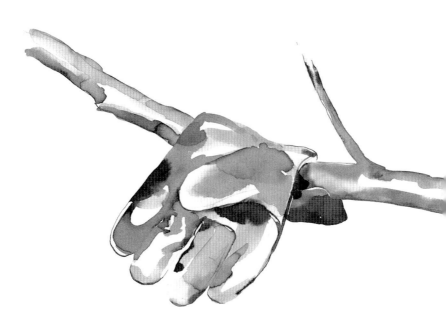

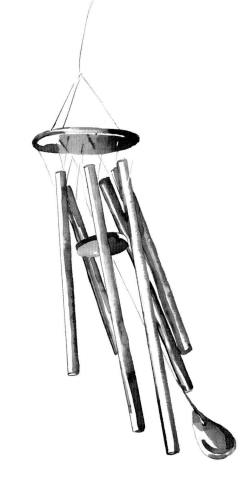

If he leaves you with a car-alarm heart,
you may learn to sing along.

It is hard to stop loving the ocean.
Even after it has left you gasping, salty.

Forgive yourself for the decisions you have made,
the ones you still call mistakes
when you tuck them in at night.

And know this.

Know you are the type of woman
who is looking for a place to call yours.

Let the statues crumble.
You have always been the place.

You are a woman who can build it yourself.
You were born to build.

[waterproof]

enough
room?

lower

tire instead?

This poem is for TG.

Acknowledgments

With utmost thanks to Sophia Janowitz, Jan Kawamura-Kay, Jeffrey Kay, PK, Sarah Wainwright, Joel Janowitz, Anne Lilly, Anna Pease, Esther Burson, Andrew Bellisari, Sofia Solomon, Cécile Garcia, Cristin O'Keefe Aptowicz, Rachel McKibbens & the Pink Door Retreat, Hedgebrook, Jacqueline Novogratz, Seth Godin, Yfat Reiss Gendell, Mauro DiPreta,

and all the women who teach me how to build.

About the Author and Illustrator

Sarah Kay is a poet from New York City who was born in 1988. She has been invited to share her poetry on such diverse stages as the 2011 TED conference; the Malthouse Theatre in Melbourne, Australia; the Royal Danish Theatre in Copenhagen, Denmark; and Carnegie Hall in New York City, among hundreds of other venues around the world. She is the author of two additional poetry books: *B* (Hachette Books) and *No Matter the Wreckage* (Write Bloody Publishing). Sarah is the founder and co-director of Project VOICE, an organization that brings spoken word poetry to schools and communities around the world.

Sophia Janowitz has created chickens out of bathmats for the New York Philharmonic at Lincoln Center, chocolate buttons for a pop-up store in Boston, a poster for a musical premiering at the Jewish Refugees Museum in Shanghai, and a cardboard levitating house for a play premiering in New York City. She is currently studying typography design in Paris.